Has anyone seen my glasses?

for:

May God bless your life abundantly
with love, joy and peace.

from:

May the LORD who created the heavens and the earth give you his blessing.

Psalm 115:15

(Contemporary English Version)

Has anyone seen my glasses... phone... car keys?

*No power in the sky above or in the earth below – indeed, nothing
in all creation will ever be able to separate us from the love of God
that is revealed in Christ Jesus our Lord.*

Romans 8:39 (NLT)

●

Is it a sign of getting older that pretty much every single day I lose something? My mobile phone has a habit of disappearing just as I'm about to leave the house, but at least someone can ring my number when I need to find it. We'll be in the car, ready to drive away, and I'll realise that my phone has gone for a walk. I rush back into the house while my daughter dials the prodigal phone from the comfort of the car. There follows much rushing up and down stairs because, although I can hear it ringing, I never seem to find it straight away.

For my mother, glasses are the biggest offender. Just as we are about to watch TV you can guarantee that she will ask, "Has anyone seen my glasses?" and then we all join the search for the runaway specs. And we always seem to find them in the very last place we look – well that stands to reason, doesn't it?

Some folk wear their glasses on a chain round their neck, but for those who have three different pairs of glasses for reading, driving and watching TV, that would be a touch ridiculous.

The London Transport Lost Property Office is given about 600 lost items a day. In one 12-month period, they received 23,432 phones, 10,632 keys, 10,150 pairs of glasses, 8,052 umbrellas, plus numerous pairs of false teeth, the urns of two dearly beloved relatives, a lawnmower, a park bench and even some breast implants – it's always good to get things off your chest! All these things were left on the tube, buses, trains or in taxis of our great capital. It's amazing how easily people can be separated from their belongings, isn't it? Sadly only one in three of these items is ever reunited with its owner.

While it's very easy to lose material things, you can never lose God's love – nothing you do can make God love you less, because he created you and loves you as his own child. And though you might forget him or turn away from him, he is always there waiting and hoping that you will return to him. Now that's worth making a note of – if you can find your glasses!

Father God, no matter how many other things we forget,
help us to always remember that your amazing love is wider than
the widest ocean and deeper than the deepest sea.
And thank you that nothing, absolutely nothing in all creation
can separate us from your immense love.

A woman walked into an optician's to return a pair of glasses that she had purchased for her husband the week before.

The assistant asked, "What seems to be the problem, Madam?"

The woman replied, "Sorry, but I'm returning these glasses that I bought for my husband. Unfortunately, he still can't see things my way."

Who put the phone in the freezer?

But Martha was distracted by the big dinner she was preparing.
Luke 10:40 (NLT)

I love my cordless phone, it enables me to multi-task. I can cook tea and phone a friend, sort the washing and call my mother, empty the bins and ring the office… The only trouble is that when I finish the call I tend to abandon the phone and carry on with the task in hand. And so it was that my poor phone got left in the freezer. I was chatting to a friend while rummaging through the frozen peas and tubs of ice cream to find inspiration for that night's supper. Reaching the end of the phone call, I left the phone on a tub of ice cream to give me two free hands to delve deeper into the freezer. I'm sure you can guess what happened next…

I usually give cold callers a frosty reception – now my frozen phone was capable of nothing but cold calling.

Multi-tasking during muddle age is not always a good idea. Sometimes we try to do too much and trip ourselves up. It reminds me of Martha who was so keen to provide the cleanest house and the best meal that she forgot to simply sit down and enjoy Jesus' company.

Sometimes we spend too much time *doing* and not enough just *being*. We attempt too much and then we have no time for ourselves, or other people, or God. It's good to remember that we're called human *beings* not human *doings* and there are times when God wants us to simply be – to sit and listen and think and to be aware of all that's happening around us – and then he will show us what to do next, and that might be nothing at all. JM

The joys and perils of multi-tasking

Father God, sometimes I attempt to do too much and get in a right muddle – remind me that there are times when it's good to be still and to spend a little quiet time with you.

You know you are getting old when...

You hear yourself passing on advice and realise you sound just like your own parents.

●

You discover that the toys you had as a child and donated to a charity shop are now worth a small fortune.

●

You remember when the screen was tiny, the cabinet was three times larger and the television took at least two minutes to warm up.

●

You find yourself with the fridge door open, gazing at the contents, wondering what on earth you wanted to get out.

●

You try to open your front door remotely by clicking the central locking key for your car.

●

You start to say something and then forget what you were about to...

●

You used to go to bed at dawn, but now that's when you get up.

●

You bend down to tie up your shoelaces and wonder what else you can do while you're down there.

●

You try to check a book out of the library with your supermarket loyalty card.

We don't stop playing because we grow old,
we grow old because we stop playing.

Anon

It's a lo-o-o-ong story!

Then you will call on me and come and pray to me, and I will listen to you.
Jeremiah 29:12 (NIV)

●

My friend, Gwen, has lived an interesting life and has some great stories to tell. Trouble is, she gets sidetracked in the telling of them and what should be a straightforward narrative ends up as a very, very lo-o-o-ong story.

"Did I ever tell you about the time I got stuck in a hot-air balloon?" she might ask.

"No," you reply, even though you've heard it at least a dozen times.

Well, before she's even become airborne, she's describing how she lost her hat at Royal Ascot in 1957, which reminds her of the particularly bad dose of flu her friend had in 2001. *That*, in turn, leads to the first time her father's cousin's neighbour tasted lobster. And so it goes on. Eventually, she'll find her way back to the hot-air balloon. Mind you, there will be numerous deviations, repetitions and hesitations before she finally lands. And *that's* where the real story begins!

My prayers can sometimes be like that. I'll start off with the intention of bringing a certain situation before God, and before I know it, I'm digressing into all kinds of unrelated territory. In fact, when I pray late at night, I have been known to fall asleep without ever mentioning what was originally on my mind.

Fortunately, God is always willing to listen to me wittering on. He's delighted when any of us want to talk to him. The fact that we seek him out and share the details of our lives with him is more important than the words we actually use. And the longer we spend talking with our Heavenly Father, the better, but if, like me, you tend to go off at wild tangents in the middle of praying, why not write down a few prayer pointers to ensure that you remember the important things?

AC

A lot of hot air!

Ah Lord, you are so patient with us! You've always got time when your children want to tell you, or ask you, something. Give us patience to listen when people want to share their stories with us. Especially if they're lo-o-o-ong stories!
Amen

University of life in Christ

Do yourself a favour and learn all you can;
then remember what you learn and you will prosper.
Proverbs 19:8 (GNT)

●

My printer and I don't see eye to eye; we often have fallings out. And as for my mobile phone… Fortunately, my daughter sorts them out whenever a problem arises. As I quite often have a problem, there's a lot of sighing on the other end of the phone when I ring her for advice.

"It's simple enough…" she assures me. She's probably right. The trouble is, I'm lazy when it comes to technology. I'm not interested in how printers and mobiles work, so I

To print or not to print

You don't have to know how the computer works, just how to work the computer.

Anon

only half listen when she explains what I need to do. I've learnt as much as I want to – such as where to locate the on-off button – and if someone's willing (albeit somewhat grudgingly) to help me when I can't do something, why make the effort to learn to do it myself?

As a Christian, it's possible to become lazy, too. You know the sort of thing I mean – *"I've read the Bible stories, been to house groups, heard countless sermons, sung the hymns, been there and bought the T-shirt. I don't feel the need to discover anything new."*

Sadly, when we think we know all there is to know about God, we close our minds to new understanding and possibilities. That attitude can be the start of a slippery slope. In order to enjoy a living relationship with God, we need to keep learning, otherwise we stagnate and our faith starts to wither.

God is bigger and far more complex than we can ever imagine. When we worship in new ways and discover 'fresh expressions' of church, then our relationship with him develops and grows and that can only be a good thing.

AC

Father God, I still have so much to discover about you.
It makes for an exciting journey.
Thank you.

Most merciful Redeemer, Friend and Brother,
may we know you more clearly,
love you more dearly,
and follow you more nearly,
day by day.
Richard of Chichester *1197–1253, English bishop*

Quips and QUOTES

Celebrity senior moments

Sir John Gielgud once told Elizabeth Taylor that Richard Burton's acting had really gone downhill after marrying *'that terrible woman'*. He had totally forgotten that the terrible woman in question was Elizabeth herself.

●

Zsa Zsa Gabor was once asked about her increasingly bad memory. *"Dahling,"* she said. *"How do you think the 'dahling' thing got started?"*

●

G.K. Chesterton, author of the *Father Brown* stories, was prone to senior moments from a young age. He once wrote a letter to his mother announcing the splendid news of his engagement to Frances, completely forgetting that his mother was in the room with him.

●

Late at night, Pope John XXIII would lie in bed thinking through serious problems and he'd say to himself, *'I really must tell the Pope about this.'* Then, he'd wake up fully and remember, *'I am the Pope.'*

●

Famous film star Doris Day was walking down the street when a man stopped her. Thinking he was a fan she greeted him politely and then walked on.
"Don't you remember me?" said the man.
"No, should I?" replied the lovely actress.
"Well you didn't have that many husbands..." replied her second husband, George Weidler.

Today is the youngest you will ever be – so have fun and act
like a child while you still can!

Out of memory

I will remember your great deeds, LORD; I will recall the wonders you did in the past.
I will think about all that you have done; I will meditate on all your mighty acts.

Psalm 77:11-12 (GNT)

•

Computers – don't you just love them? Well, perhaps not always. Sometimes I find them quite incomprehensible, but then I can still recall the dark ages PC (as in Pre-Computers). I can remember a time when a keyboard was a piano, a mouse was a furry rodent, a virus was the flu, a hard drive was a long car journey, a cursor was someone who used swear words, the web was a spider's home and memory was something you lost as you grew older...

Last week, I was happily tapping away on my keyboard when a message popped up on my screen. **Out of memory**. *'Well...'* I thought, *'I know just how you feel.'* I often struggle to remember things – the name of a neighbour, the birthday of a friend, that foreign town I visited on holiday last year.

Sometimes I test my memory – how many school friends can I name in my ancient class photo, how many birthdays can I reel off without looking them up and, if my mind wanders during the sermon, how many members of the congregation can I name, and their children and their pets. It's all good brain training!

The words of David's psalm above remind us that we can also challenge ourselves to remember all the good things that God has done for us, this past week... this last year. If we feel worried about the future, or concerned about a new challenge – it's encouraging to remember all that God has done in the past, to make a mental list of the many blessings we have received, and before long the future doesn't look half so terrifying.

JM

Lord, please help me to remember all the good things you have done for me in the past, all the ways you have helped me to overcome problems and difficulties and then remind me that you will be at my side as I face tomorrow.

The joys of technology

User error: replace user and press any key to continue.

●

To err is human, but to really mess things up requires a computer.

●

Computers are so disappointing – I keep hitting 'escape' – but I'm still here.

Selective memory

I will forgive their sins and I will no longer remember their wrongs.
Jeremiah 31:34 (GNT)

I deserve an A* GCSE in forgetting things. I can stand in front of the fridge with the door open and not remember what I intended to get out. I can go to the supermarket to buy milk and come out with ten other things and no milk. And I can hide all the Christmas presents I buy in October, but when it's time to wrap them in December I can't find my own secret hiding place.

And then there are all the times when I forget people's names, though I have found a solution to that problem. Just call everyone 'there'. If you see someone in the street and can't remember their name, simply smile and wave and say, "Hello there!"

Yes, I admit it – I have a highly developed 'forgetory'. How about you?

Did you know that squirrels and chipmunks are probably even more forgetful than humans? Every year they bury hundreds and thousands of acorns, nuts and seeds to provide food for the winter months and then they promptly forget where they've hidden them. Over the years the shortfall in their long-term memory is responsible for the planting of millions of new trees, which is great for our environment – sometimes good things come from forgetfulness.

God himself is also forgetful. That's hard to believe, isn't it? But there are many things that God deliberately forgets – he has a selective memory. When we turn to him and ask forgiveness for all our wrongdoing, God chooses not only to forgive us, but also to forget all our sin. In fact, he throws it as far away as possible...

You will trample our sins underfoot and send them to the bottom of the sea!
Micah 7:19 (GNT)

Now that's an image that's too good to forget.　JM

Red squirrels: Charles Kinsey

Lord, thank you for forgetting all those times when I have hurt you or made you feel sad. Let me never forget your gift of love and forgiveness.

You know you are getting old when...

You feel a sense of triumph when you remember what you came upstairs for
– without first having to go back downstairs.

The phone rings and you answer the television remote control.

Pension plans take over as a favourite topic of conversation.

Your new car cost as much as your first house.

You could legally marry someone half your age
– and they in turn could legally marry someone half their age.

In your opinion, a good night out is a quiet night in.

Someone gives you a measurement in metric and you convert it back to
feet and inches.

You believe that pacemakers are a pop band headed by a man called Gerry.

Count your age by friends, not years.
Count your life by smiles, not tears.
John Lennon 1940–1980,
English singer, songwriter and member of the Beatles

You are never too old to sing in the rain
and dance in the puddles.

Singing – and dancing – in the rain

19

He's got the whole world in His hands

Who else has held the oceans in his hand?
Who has measured off the heavens with his fingers?
Who else knows the weight of the earth
or has weighed the mountains and hills on a scale?

Isaiah 40:12 (NLT)

•

Every American President is accompanied by an armed guard with a titanium briefcase containing the nuclear launch codes, while the president himself carries a special identity key in his pocket that has to be used in conjunction with the codes. It's a good system, but even the leader of the free world has an occasional senior moment. Can you guess which President left the vital key in his suit jacket and sent it to the dry cleaners? Is *peanut farmer* a big enough clue? The mind boggles doesn't it – is the world really safe in the hands of any single human being?

As I child, I used to enjoy singing the chorus,

He's got the whole world in His hands. He's got you and me, brother, in His hands,

He's got you and me, sister, in His hands, He's got the whole world in His hands.

I used to imagine an enormous pair of kind hands cradling the world. It was a reassuring image, though it made God seem like the BFG – Big Friendly Giant.

The lyrics remind us that God created every square inch of our world – from the sun and moon, wind and rain, hill and valley, right down to the 'little bitty baby'. Our planet is his much loved creation and that includes every single human being on it. We are his children and when we put our lives in the Father's hands, he then invites us to become his hands here on earth, to show his love, care and compassion to the world, and to do his work on earth.

So what do you have planned for today? Why not ask the Father if he has a special job for your hands to do?

Christ has no body but yours,
No hands, no feet on earth but yours,
Yours are the eyes with which he looks
Compassion on this world,
Yours are the feet with which he walks to do good,
Yours are the hands, with which he blesses all the world.

Teresa of Ávila 1515–1582, Spanish Carmelite nun

View from the hill: Greta Chang

Father God, take my hands, take my feet, and let them work for you.

Power of attorney

God cares for you, so turn all your worries over to him.
1 Peter 5:7 (CEV)

"I don't have to worry about forgetting to pay my gas and electric bill or understanding any mumbo jumbo letters," my neighbour, Wilf told me. "My son, David, has got power of attorney. He sees to all that for me. It's marvellous!" he smiled as he dead-headed another rose.

He may be old and a bit forgetful at times, and he does need a mobility scooter to get around, but Wilf certainly isn't daft. He was only too ready to let his son take care of all the complicated financial, legal and administrative business when David offered. He's got fewer things to worry about now. He can enjoy his old age and his roses, safe in the knowledge that someone capable and willing has taken charge.

Jesus offers us the opportunity to entrust the ordering of our lives to him. He doesn't want us worrying about the future. The last thing he wants is for us to be casting fearful glances over our shoulder at every turn. He wants us to be free to enjoy the good things God created – fragrant roses, awesome landscapes, lovable animals, warm sunshine, good food and one another – safe in the knowledge that he is in charge and has our best interests at heart.

When we give him our heart, he works with us and for us in the name of all that is holy. Of course, he wants the best for us anyway, but it's only when we give him the equivalent of 'power of attorney' that he can have the biggest impact on our lives. When we share our worries with him, he will show us the best path to take and will be with us every step of the way, ensuring we don't trip. And we can rest assured that our cares are no burden to him.

The future is bright when the Lord takes charge of the controls!

*Oh Jesus, what a friend we have in you.
It's a relief to give my worries to you and it means that
I feel more able to stop and smell the roses. Thank you!*

Raindrops on roses: Judith Merrell

Pray, and let God worry.
Martin Luther 1483–1546, German priest and professor of theology

If growing up means it would be beneath my dignity to climb a tree,
I'll never grow up, never grow up, never grow up! Not me!

J.M. Barrie 1860–1937, *Scottish author of* Peter Pan

Quips and QUOTES

Celebrity chat

Men are like wine – some turn to vinegar, but the best improve with age.
Pope John XXIII 1881–1963

●

The advantage of a bad memory is that one enjoys several times
the same good things for the first time.
Friedrich Nietzsche 1844–1900, German philosopher

●

I just don't think of age and time in respect of years. I have too much experience of
people in their seventies who are vigorous and useful and people who are thirty-five
who are in lousy physical shape and can't think straight. I don't think age has that
much to do with it.
Harrison Ford born 1942, American actor

●

Getting older is fabulous. The longer you do it the more technique you acquire.
That makes the game easier.
Cherie Lunghi born 1952, English actress

●

The secret of staying young is to live honestly, eat slowly, and lie about your age.
Lucille Ball 1911–1989, American actress and comedian

●

One should never trust a woman who tells one her real age.
A woman who would tell one that would tell one anything.
Oscar Wilde 1854–1900, Irish writer

Carry me!

*Carry each other's burdens, and in this way
you will fulfil the law of Christ.*
Galatians 6:2 (NIV)

●

We were having a late family holiday in the Lake District. We enjoy going out of season in the colder weather. There's something special about the landscape when the trees have dropped their leaves. We were walking, my wife Barbara, two daughters and husbands, and four grandchildren.

Georgia, the youngest, is a good walker, very determined, and rarely complains. But after a succession of rough paths she was tired. "Carry me, Daddy" and up she went on his shoulders. I wished he could have done the same for me – paths seem to get steeper these days – and my knees aren't what they used to be.

We all need a carry at times. Not literally, I'd look a fool perched on my son-in-law's back. But now and then, particularly in winter, life can seem to stand still and we feel we're living in a monochrome, monotonous world. That's when we need the encouragement of a friend, a sympathetic listener. Someone who'll help carry us along. And the best way to find one? By giving someone else the lift and encouragement they need today. Then maybe, when the lights go to red in your life, there'll be someone around to share your feelings and give you the support you need.

*Lord, sometimes my burdens seem too heavy
and my energy too light.
But if you'll take the other end I'll try to lift my share.*

Eddie Askew *1927–2007, Christian writer and former International Director of The Leprosy Mission, taken from* Chasing the Leaves

Flying high

Anything you can do...

But as the scripture says,
"Whoever wants to boast must boast about what the Lord has done."
2 Corinthians 10:17 (GNT)

●

The competition is stiff when the senior residents of Cable Close meet for their monthly chinwag over lunch. You'd normally associate such showing off with a classroom of primary school children, but these young pensioners would beat any group of youngsters, hands down.

And what do these gentlefolk claim superiority in? Medical matters. Who's been to the doctor's surgery the most times in the past month; who takes the most pills; who's in the most pain; who has the highest cholesterol; who most needs a knee replacement; or who has survived the most life-threatening operations. Yes, I exaggerate, but only a teeny bit!

But perhaps I'm being a little unfair. Young or old, we're all competitive to a degree, and once our ability to play fast sports, take part in advanced chess tournaments or do cryptic crosswords and so on has lost its edge, there's a limit to the areas left where we can compete with one another. As one old fellow commented, "The only sport left to me now is hunting for my glasses!"

Competition, regardless of age and ability, isn't necessarily a bad thing. It's good to challenge our minds and push our bodies, as long as we recognise that coming out tops isn't the be-all and end-all. And, that we remember to thank God for our moments of triumph, remembering that every success is a celebration of our God-given abilities.

If we feel tempted to 'boast', let it be with regard to the freedom we have in Christ and the blessings he has bestowed upon us all. And let's tell of God's extravagant creativity and goodness.

It's good to laugh!

Lord God, You alone are worthy to receive glory and honour and praise.
I want to boast of your goodness in – and to – the whole world!

Quips and QUOTES
Medical muddle

*Sometimes doctors suffer from muddle-age and make the most confusing notes.
Here are some actual statements taken from medical records
written by various paramedics and doctors...*

●

The patient had waffles for breakfast and anorexia for lunch.

●

The baby was delivered, the cord clamped and cut and handed to the
paediatrician who breathed and cried immediately.

●

I saw your patient today, who is still under our car for physical therapy.

●

The patient lives at home with his mother,
father, and pet turtle, who is presently enrolled
in day care three times a week.

●

While in the emergency room, she was
examined, X-rated and sent home.

●

The skin was moist and dry.

●

Patient was alert and unresponsive.

●

When she fainted, her eyes
rolled around the room.

Discharge status: Alive but without permission.

Patient has left his white blood cells at another hospital.

The patient's past medical history has been remarkably insignificant with only a 40 pound weight gain in the past three days.

She slipped on the ice and apparently her legs went in separate directions in early December.

Patient has chest pains if she lies on her left side for over a year.

By the time he was admitted, his rapid heart had stopped and he was feeling much better.

The patient is a 79-year-old widow who no longer lives with her husband.

The patient refused an autopsy.

Poor old Ted

Out of sight, out of mind

LORD, I call to you for help; every morning I pray to you.
Psalm 88:13 (GNT)

●

The plan was simple enough. While the eggs were boiling, I'd nip upstairs with the basket of freshly ironed laundry. I'd just about have time to put it away before the eggs were done.

I'd got as far as putting clean towels in the bathroom when I noticed that the toilet roll needed replacing and then I stopped to rescue a spider from the bath. At this point my mobile rang. The car was ready to be picked up from the garage. Good. A quick call to my husband at work to let him know. Then a call to a friend to let her know I *would* now be able to give her a lift to the meeting at church. Needless to say, that call took longer than planned as we chatted about anything and everything.

It was 20 minutes later when I finally got around to putting the rest of the laundry away. Funny, was that next door's smoke alarm going? It sounded unusually close. In fact, I could even smell whatever it was they were burning. Reminded me a bit of... *eggs!*

Abandoning shirts and socks, I rushed downstairs. The smoke detector was still screeching its *eggs-boiled-dry-in-the-bottom-of-the-pan* warning as I grabbed the saucepan and filled it with water from the tap. It was too late to save the eggs for the salad I had planned. Still, the dogs thoroughly enjoyed them. What a yolk!

I know what you are thinking – that this was just another senior moment, but I'm putting this mishap down to being egg-stremely busy. Sometimes we all have days that are so hectic we chase round like the legendary headless chicken. Some folk find it helps to spend time with Jesus at the beginning of the day asking him to help them prioritise the tasks on the 'To do' list. After all, young or old, there are only so many plates we can spin before, as sure as eggs is eggs, they come crashing to the ground.

Lord, sometimes we can be over-ambitious.
Show me which things are important and how to spend my time wisely.

If your day is hemmed in with prayer, it is less likely to come unravelled.

Anon

Every Christian needs a half-hour of prayer each day, except when he is busy, then he needs an hour.

Francis de Sales *1567-1622, Bishop of Geneva.*

Quick question: Is there a GPS that will help teenagers find the laundry basket?

Happiness is... a basketful of clean laundry

The basic ingredients

Once there were ten young women who took their oil lamps and went out to meet the bridegroom. Five of them were foolish, and the other five were wise. The foolish ones took their lamps but did not take any extra oil with them, while the wise ones took containers full of oil for their lamps.

Matthew 25:1–4 (GNT)

●

Brenda's friends would be arriving in just under an hour. The meat and potatoes were in the oven, the veg was prepared, the pudding ready and the table laid. Brenda was ahead of schedule. In fact, she had enough time to whip up a cake for tea. It wasn't part of the original plan, but the oven was hot and it would only take ten minutes to make. She'd strike while the iron was hot and show her guests that, despite her advancing years, she still had plenty of get up and go.

Brenda weighed out the sugar and margarine and started beating. In went the eggs. Humming as she worked, she reached in the cupboard for the flour and that's when she came unstuck. The cupboard was bare, at least in terms of flour. So much for her impromptu baking. She put the mixture in the fridge and added 'flour' to her shopping list.

It's easy to get carried away when we're 'on a roll'. A wave of enthusiasm can be wonderful, but we can sometimes find ourselves out of our depth. Planning and preparation may be boring and irksome but they can save a lot of hassle and heartache in the long run. As they say in business: *Failing to plan is planning to fail.*

Our spiritual store cupboard should also be stocked with the basic ingredients: the Word of God in the form of regular Bible reading, a willingness to listen and serve, and a readiness to pray. Equipped with these, we will be ready for anything – planned or unplanned.

AC

What a yolk!

*Lord, help me to stay in tune with the plans you have for me
and help me to be ready for the day ahead,
equipped to tackle the tasks you give me.*

Life begins at retirement – goodbye tension, hello pension.

Reclining in a tree: Helen Sharpe

Quips and **QUOTES**

The joy of retirement

The money is certainly no better in retirement, but the hours are!

•

The downside to retirement is having to drink coffee in your own time.

•

When a man retires and time is no longer a matter of urgent importance,
his colleagues generally present him with a watch.

R.C. Sherriff 1896–1975, English playwright

•

When you retire at 65 you are not so very old
because if there were 15 months in every year you'd only be 52.

•

It is time I stepped aside for a less experienced and less able man.

Scott Elledge 1914–1997, American Professor of English Literature

•

I enjoy waking up and not having to go to work.
So I do it three or four times a day.

Gene Perret born 1937, American comedy writer

•

Retirement at sixty-five is ridiculous. When I was sixty-five I still had pimples.

George Burns 1896–1996, American comedian

•

A retired husband is often a wife's full-time job.

Ella Harris, Author

School reports

So encourage each other and build each other up, just as you are already doing.
1 Thessalonians 5:11 (NLT)

●

My mother has reached that age in life when decluttering is top of her agenda and so on her last visit she gave me a big folder of papers. I put it away and forgot about it, because I'm at the age where hiding the clutter is my number one priority. Weeks later, I found the folder and discovered all my old school reports...

There was my infant school teacher who commended my *'brave attempts at spelling'* – that's a nice way to put it. And another teacher who said my singing was *'good but a bit erratic'*. I'm actually tone deaf, but at least she didn't write me off completely. Then, there was my secondary school geography teacher who wrote, *'Judith has ability, but she hasn't used it this year in this subject.'* Succinctly put.

A Munich school teacher once told the young Albert Einstein: *'You will never amount to very much.'* He was only ten at the time, I wonder how he felt? Today, Einstein is the nickname given to the class genius, I hope that school teacher has eaten his words.

In other school reports, John Lennon was declared to be *'hopeless... rather a clown in class... certainly on the road to failure'*; while Gary Lineker's teacher warned: *'He must devote less of his time to sport if he wants to be a success – you can't make a living out of football.'*

Going further back in history, Charlotte Brontë was told that she wrote *'indifferently'* and *'knew nothing of grammar'*. What an encouragement for anyone struggling with English Literature today.

Looking back on my school days, I can see who encouraged me and who did quite the opposite. When we're young, we have big dreams and splendid plans for our future – some adults encourage us, but sadly others put us down. Reading back over my school reports, I was struck by the fact that if I liked the teacher, I liked the subject they taught and tried hard, but if I didn't like the teacher then sadly that subject became a lost cause.

Children and adults need encouragement just the way a plant needs water, and you don't have to be a teacher to encourage others, whether they are young, old or somewhere in the middle. Ask yourself what you can do to spread a little joy and encouragement today – then go ahead and do it. *JM*

Father God, help me to be ready with a kind word or an encouraging comment to bring your love into the world around me.

Television presenter, Jon Snow, found the following comment on his school report:
"Jon has set himself low standards, which he has failed to live up to."

Off to school

Time for tea

I will refresh those who are weary...
Jeremiah 31:25 (GNT)

●

"I *need* a cup of tea!" I declared, arriving home after a trip into town.

I was cringing, even as the words left my mouth. You see, I was never going to go down the *'I-could-do-with-a-nice-cup-of-tea'* road. As a child, I could

Tea for two: Tim Sandall

Wouldn't it be dreadful to live in a country where they didn't have tea?
Noel Coward *1899–1973, English playwright and actor*

never understand the adults' obsession with tea. Especially when they tried convincing me it was more refreshing than a cold drink on a hot day. Nonsense!

Well, time has passed and now I'm a believer! A cup of char works wonders. It's calming, comforting and restorative. Hot and bothered? Put the kettle on. Had a shock? Put the kettle on. Feeling low or under the weather? Put the kettle on. Not sure what to do? Stick the kettle on.

I find it hard to believe I used to turn my nose up at this great cure-all. But then, I find it hard to believe I used to turn my nose up at Christianity.

Of course, wise people entrust their lives to God at a young age. They know a good thing when they see it, or should I say the Good News when they hear it. Others fight the call to faith for all, or most of, their lives, determined that they don't need the Father's help.

Once we become Christians, we appreciate the benefits of turning to Jesus in each and every situation. Like tea, he is calming, comforting and restorative. Unlike tea, which only refreshes until we are thirsty again, his word is 'the water of life' and endures forever.

In the words of the hymn*:
> 'I heard the voice of Jesus say, "Come unto Me and rest..."
> I came to Jesus, and I drank of that life-giving stream;
> My thirst was quenched, my soul revived, and now I live in Him.'

That says it all really!

AC

*Father, thank you that we can find rest and refreshment
when we spend time with you.
Help us to make it a daily event.*

* by **Horatius Bonar** 1808–1889, Church of Scotland Minister

Quips and
QUOTES
Crazy Claims

*These folk were evidently suffering from advanced muddle-age
when they filled in their insurance claims...*

•

Going to work at 7 a.m. this morning I drove out of my drive straight into a bus.
The bus was five minutes early.

•

I started to slow down but the traffic was more stationary than I thought.

•

On approach to the traffic lights the car in front suddenly broke.

•

I collided with a stationary truck coming the other way.

•

The other car collided with mine without giving warning of its intention.

•

In an attempt to kill a fly, I drove into a telephone pole.

•

I told the police that I was not injured, but on removing my hat found that
I had a fractured skull.

•

No one was to blame for the accident, but it would never have happened
if the other driver had been alert.

•

I bumped into a lamp-post which was obscured by human beings.

Just smile and wave!

The accident was caused by me waving to the man I hit last week.

I didn't think the speed limit applied after midnight.

Lasting love

God showed how much he loved us by sending his one and only Son into the world so that we might have eternal life through him.

1 John 4:9 (NLT)

●

The hassled lady at the front of the queue packed all her groceries away, then popped her handbag down and rummaged for her bank cards. The check-out assistant smiled and looked puzzled... "Do you always carry your television remote control in your handbag?" she asked. "No, not usually," said the harassed shopper. "I asked my husband to help with the shopping, but he refused so I figured this was the best way to get my own back!" Love and marriage, eh? I wonder if that couple exchanged Valentine cards this year.

Watching the local news, I heard about one wife who finally received her first Valentine card after 65 years. The couple met at a dance in a church hall when Joyce was 15 and she married Fred three years later. But in all the years since, Fred has never bought her a single Valentine card, bunch of flowers or even a box of chocolates.

"This card is a lovely surprise," grinned Joyce. "I think I'll frame it. Though I never felt hard done by, because actions speak louder than words. He'd tell me *"I love you"* every day and I'd get a kiss... I can't grumble. And we had a lovely marriage. The secret is to keep saying "Yes, dear," added Joyce with a chuckle.

When God wanted to tell us how much he loved us, he sent us something far better than a Valentine card, he sent his very own son, whose actions spoke louder than any words. Jesus stretched out his arms to say *"I love you this much"* and then he accepted the punishment for all we've done wrong, so that we could be forgiven. And now Jesus invites us to enjoy eternal life with him – and that's our very own *match made in heaven.*

With heartfelt love

*Lord, many Valentine cards end with a row of loving crosses xxx,
but your immense love starts with the cross.
Thank you.*

So... where did I park the car?

Mistaken identity

If you look for me wholeheartedly, you will find me.
Jeremiah 29:13 (NLT)

●

Having 'lost' my car on more than one occasion, I made sure I remembered *exactly* where I parked this time. There'd be no heart-stopping moments today. No trawling the rows of vehicles in search of my motor.

Except that when I returned to the spot, laden with groceries, my car wasn't there. I looked around, my heart racing. There was the red sports car I'd parked next to, and there was the gorse bush, shaped like a fat rabbit, I'd lined up with. This time, someone really *had* stolen my vehicle!

After checking line upon line of cars (in case I'd remembered wrongly), I started punching my home phone number into my mobile. Terry would have to come and pick me up in the van. Ah. The van. The *van*. I turned to where I'd parked and there was *the van* – not *the car* – exactly where I'd left it.

I'm guessing that I'm not the only one who can't find something because it bears no resemblance to what I *think* I'm looking for? Little wonder then, that we sometimes convince ourselves God has gone AWOL – or was never there to begin with. Perhaps we've forgotten what God is like, or our idea of him is so far removed from his reality, that we don't recognise his constant presence in our lives. Some folk find it hard to detect God's presence in troubled times, but he is right there beside us even in the most difficult situations.

God is more caring and more interested in us than we ever dare imagine. Not sure how or where to find him? Ask the Father to make himself known to you. Sometimes, it's more a case of standing still and allowing yourself to be *found by him*. AC

How many times have I missed you, Lord, because I was looking for
my own idea of you, rather than the real you? You are the one true God,
way beyond all I could ever imagine or hope for.
Help me to recognise your presence in my life.

Quips and QUOTES

Academics never get old, they just lose their faculties.

Accountants never get old, they just lose their balance.

Bakers never get old, they just knead a rest.

Bank managers never get old, they just lose interest.

Dentists never get old, just a bit long in the tooth.

Doctors never get old, they just lose their patience.

Electricians never get old, they just lose their spark.

Engineers never get old, they just lose their bearings.

Golfers never get old, they just lose their drive.

Hairdressers never get old, they might curl up, but they refuse to dye.

Printers never get old, they're just not the type.

Racing drivers never get old, they just go round the bend.

Sculptors never get old, they just lose their marbles.

Teachers never get old, they just mark time.

Vehicle mechanics never get old, they just re-tyre every day.

Vets never get old, they just get dog-tired.

Watchmakers never get old, they just wind down.

Garden roller: Richard Ward

Farmers never get old, they just go to seed.

Gardeners never get old, they just go to pot.

Absent-minded

The Spirit will teach you everything and will remind you of what I said
while I was with you.
John 14:26 (CEV)

●

I've just put my car keys in the office fridge. No, it wasn't an accident, I did it quite deliberately. You see, sometimes I pop out at lunchtime and buy some bits and pieces from the supermarket and more than once I've gone home leaving behind the essential ingredients for supper. My friend, Helen, mentioned that in her office they pop their car keys in the fridge so they won't forget their shopping. It's a great idea and it works pretty well. Although yesterday I spent a few minutes hunting high and low for my keys, before remembering that they were chilling out in the fridge!

When it comes to remembering things, I need all the help I can get. I often go upstairs to fetch something, but then have to return downstairs to remember what it is? I regularly open the microwave to find the cup of coffee I was reheating yesterday still languishing inside. And sometimes I start telling a joke and then realise that I can't remember the punch line. Life is busy, there are tons of distractions and remembering things is tough.

Jesus knew that the trauma of the crucifixion and the excitement of the resurrection would probably make the disciples forget everything that he had told them. And so he reassured them that the Holy Spirit would come as a helper and remind them of the important things he said during his time with them – you can read Jesus' promise at the top of the page.

For Christians today, the Holy Spirit is like an 'interior teacher' prompting us to share our faith, reminding us of Jesus' words and helping us to pray. Pope Francis describes the Holy Spirit as *'the living memory of the church'* – helping us to recall Jesus' words in our hearts so they become part of us, part of our attitudes, part of our choices and testimony. And that's an excellent explanation – definitely worth remembering.

Absent-minded violinist, Philippe Quint, left his 290-year-old Stradivarius in the back of a taxi. Fortunately, the driver traced him and returned it – the violin is worth an estimated £2.5 million!

●

When Martin van Buren, the 8th President of the United States, wrote his autobiography he completely forgot to mention his wife, Hannah, the mother of his four children. Now that's top level absent-mindedness!

A cool way to remember things

Lord, thank you for understanding how easily we forget things.
And thank you for your Holy Spirit who reminds us daily
of your life and love.

Our state-of-the-art God

I praise you because I am fearfully and wonderfully made;
your works are wonderful, I know that full well.

Psalm 139:14. (NIV)

The world at our fingertips

Press ANY key to start. Hmm... where is the ANY key?

Did you know that there are two key signs of getting older? The first is loss of memory and I simply can't remember the other one...

My friend Richard used to pride himself on his memory. He was able to remember birthdays, phone numbers and addresses without needing to consult his diary or address book. But that was when he was a younger man. Now he has to write down new details or he's sunk. He can still remember his uncle's first car registration number, but ask him his daughter's address and he has to look it up.

The human brain is an ingenious piece of apparatus. It's like a computer, recording, processing and storing information. When we're young, the 'database' is relatively empty and there's tons of storage space. As we learn more, the available space decreases. With so much information stashed away, it's little wonder it takes a while to recall facts once we reach a certain age. There's a lot to sift through!

Some folk believe computers were invented in Bible times – after all Eve had an Apple and Moses used a tablet. And we can all agree that the computer is a marvellous invention, but the human brain is even more amazing. God created us with an incredible capacity to input, process, store and recall information. And it's not just mankind that's blessed with such 'technology'. He made animals and birds with in-built 'Sat Nav', enabling them to travel thousands of miles without the aid of maps or the need to stop and ask for directions.

Technology advances at a tremendous pace. But isn't it amazing to think it's only just *beginning* to catch up with the systems God put in place when he created the world in the year dot? Wherever man goes, God was there first.

AC

Creator God, I put my trust in you, confident that you are way ahead of anything man can invent or achieve. You have the safest hands and the keenest mind in the universe.

Quips and QUOTES

Political senior moments...

Some politicians only have to open their mouths to put their foot right in it!
Can you guess which politician made the following remarks?
Answer on page 55.

●

My job is a decision-making job, and as a result, I make a lot of decisions.

●

Our enemies are innovative and resourceful, and so are we. They never stop thinking about new ways to harm our country and our people, and neither do we.

●

I think we agree – the past is over.

●

The problem with the French is that they don't have a word for 'entrepreneur'.

●

I'm sure you can imagine it's an unimaginable honour to live here.

●

Rarely is the question asked: *Is our children learning?*

●

If you say you're going to do something and don't do it, that's trustworthiness.

●

You teach a child to read, and he or her will be able to pass a literacy test.

●

On visiting Denmark: I'm looking forward to a good night's sleep on the soil of a friend.

Answer: George Bush, 43rd President of the United States from 2001 to 2009

Health and safety

Have I not commanded you? Be strong and courageous. Do not be afraid;
do not be discouraged, for the LORD your God will be with you wherever you go.
Joshua 1:9 (NIV)

●

Many years ago, I was a girl guide. And with guiding comes the joy of summer camps, sleeping under canvas and spiders in your sleeping bag. Every year we would load all our stuff into the back of a removal lorry. Pots and pans and tent poles went in first, next the tents and rucksacks, and last of all our blankets and pillows to make comfortable seating. Finally, all the guides would pile in on top and we'd drive off to camp with the back doors open at the top so we could see the passing scenery.

A week under canvas

We'd take it in turns to stand in a row at the tailgate and wave at the cars behind. The journey took over an hour and we loved every minute of the trip, bouncing around in the back of the lorry without a care in the world! Looking back, it's a wonder our parents let us go! Imagine the chaos if the driver had made an emergency stop. And just imagine the risk assessment forms you'd have to fill in today...

Back in 'ye olden days' we had no seat belts, no air bags and no childproof medicine bottles – it's amazing that we've all survived to reach muddle-age isn't it? Life was hazardous in the good old days.

I'm so glad that we are more safety conscious today – although sometimes health and safety regulations go a step too far. Apparently, one in six schools has banned conkers from the playground for fear of broken wrists. Meanwhile, in one Cheshire town, the white goalposts have been removed from a playing field in case someone runs into them and a Cotswold school has taken meatballs off the menu in case a pupil chokes.

We smile and shake our heads at these crazy rules, but I have to admit to a little sympathy with the folk who instigated them. You see, as I grow older, I worry more and more about anything and everything. First, I find myself worrying about any new adventure that my teens embark upon. Driving lessons are currently top of the list. My son's away at University and he hasn't phoned recently – is he OK? And what about my mother, is she safe coming home in the dark?... Before anxiety gets a grip, I have to remind myself that God loves and cares about my family even more than I do and then ask him to watch over them, or I would never let them leave the house!

And would I let my daughter go to guide camp in the back of a lorry – never in a million years!

JM

Father God, let all our worries ensure that we take sensible precautions and make wise decisions, but once that's done help us to trust you for the rest.

All God's creatures

How many are your works, LORD! In wisdom you made them all;
the earth is full of your creatures.

Psalm 104:24 (NIV))

●

I went to the vet the other day. Not for myself – I'm not quite as disillusioned with the National Health Service as that – I took one of our dogs. While I was waiting I picked up a leaflet – 'Caring for Elderly Dogs'.

The leaflet began by describing old dogs and the more I read, the more it sounded like me. *'Greying round the muzzle'* – yes, that's me. *'Changes in body shape'* – I'm afraid so. *'Stiffness in the joints'* – certainly in my knees. *'Reluctance to take exercise'* – yes, I admit it. *'Bladder problems'* … I'll stop right there otherwise it might get a bit too personal. And I know people say that dog owners get to look like their pets but that's taking it a bit far.

It made me think though. The similarities remind me that we humans are as much a part of God's creation as anything else, and if we realised that, we might begin to treat the earth and other living things a bit differently.

Of course we are different from animals in some ways – in being able to talk, to think, to imagine. And in our feelings for the spiritual. To wonder what life is about, and to realise there's more to it than just what we can see and measure. And that more is God, who created you and me, and my dogs, and wants the best for all of us.

Major takes a swim: Brian Cartwright

And if we can begin to take that into account we may find it easier to live in harmony
with each other, the world about us, and with the God who made us.

Eddie Askew, *taken from* Slower than Butterflies

*Creator God, thank you for the awe-inspiring world you have given us;
help us to treat it with the same loving care that you offer us.*

If having a soul means being able to feel love and loyalty and gratitude,
then animals are better off than a lot of humans.

James Herriot 1916–1995, Scottish vet and author